STEAM-POWERED

FD

ADVENTURES

Copyright 2023 Experience Delicious, LLC.
ISBN: 978-1-947001-71-8
www.kidfoodexplorers.com

STEAM-POWERED

Food Adventures

101+ Child-Led Explorations for Curious Kids

Written by
Dani Lebovitz
MS, RDN

Illustrated by
Mary Navarro

To my girly-pies,

You are my inspiration. May your paths always be led by wonder, your experiments fueled by an unbounded imagination, and your days be filled with playful exploration. Your creativity lights the way on this journey of '*you choose your adventures in food*.' So, grab your Food Explorer hats! It's time to embark on this STEAM Powered Food Adventure together - let's make it deliciously fun!

"I think, at a child's birth, if a mother could ask a fairy godmother to endow it with the most useful gift, that gift would be curiosity."

—Eleanor Roosevelt

WELCOME PARENTS and EDUCATORS!

Get ready for a colorful adventure that will transform how you and your kids explore food and nutrition.

Early childhood is a time of curiosity and wonder. Lifelong habits and worldviews are shaped through every experience.

Our mission is to transform food into a playground of learning by championing a child-centered approach to food education that fosters future innovators.

WHY THIS BOOK MATTERS:

Nutrition education around health that categorizes food using dichotomous language such a 'good' or 'bad' can be harmful to how children learn about food and their bodies. This book presents a research-based framework rooted in early childhood development, emphasizing social emotional learning and cultural competency.

Integrating a STEAM (Science, Technology, Engineering, Arts, and Math) approach into food education invites active learning opportunities through meaningful hands-on experiences both inside and outside the conventional classroom setting.

WHY STEAM?

Food and nutrition naturally intersect with STEAM disciplines. They nurture critical thinking, imaginative inquiry, and problem solving skills. A STEAM approach seamlessly integrates into core curriculum and daily life, offering real-world applications that contribute to a broader understanding of the world.

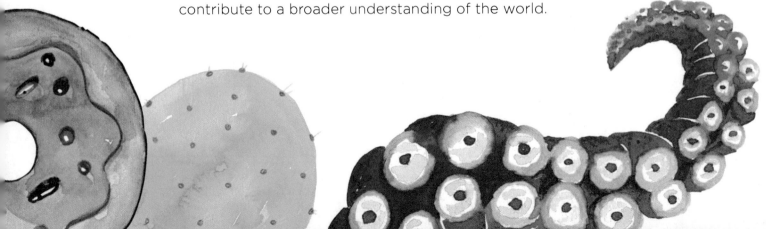

THE STEAM DIFFERENCE:

- **Child-centered:** Fosters a growth mindset, autonomy, self-worth, and self-confidence.

- **Food Positivity:** Cultivates a healthy food relationship through non-judgmental language, diverse food experiences, and interactive play.

- **Inclusivity:** Embraces children as unique individuals, valuing their interests, and celebrating diversity in foods, cultures, and abilities.

- **Skill Development:** Nurtures inquiry, creativity, critical thinking, problem-solving, and effective communication.

HOW TO USE THIS BOOK:

Imagine this book as a toolbox for inspiring child-led activities that turn food discovery into an adventure.

- **No one-size-fits-all:** This book sparks ideas, not instructions. Explore freely!

- **Start Small:** Find food-specific inspiration in color-themed pages or explore STEAM disciplines based on your child's interests.

- **Follow your child's lead:** Investigate how flowers turn into fruits, build a tower out of marshmallows and spaghetti, and make a cornhusk doll...

Explore the magic of food discovery with your child as your guide. Tell them, *"you choose your adventures in food!"*

Visit our Adventure Toolbox™ at
www.kidfoodexplorers.com
to download printables and resources.

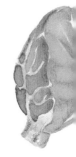

WELCOME, FOOD EXPLORER!

A *STEAM-Powered Food Adventure* is your passport to becoming a

- 🥄 kitchen wizard
- 🔍 food detective
- 🥟 food builder
- 🖌 food artist
- 📕 food math magician
- 💡 and decision-maker all at once!

This book is bursting with exciting activity inspirations, ready to uncover a world of amazing food mysteries and surprises.

WHAT WILL YOU FIND INSIDE?

🖐 Hands-on activity ideas to discover new things about food and the world around you.

🌈 A rainbow of colorful food pages bursting with investigative inspiration.

🧂 Cool facts that even grown-ups might not know.

YOUR ADVENTURE, YOUR WAY

This is your invitation to get curious and play with food!

❤ Do you love to draw and paint? You can turn your food into art!

❓ Do you like asking "Why?" or "How?" You can become a food scientist!

⚙ Love to build? Try making a castle out of food!

You choose your adventures in food - your interests and curiosity lead the way!

WHAT IS STEAM?

Have you ever wondered why apples turn brown when we cut them, how we can make a cupcake look pretty with frosting, or how many raspberries are in a plastic clamshell? Well, you are already using the power of STEAM to explore food.

Is for science, like being a kitchen detective, discovering why food does amazing things, such as how ice cream freezes or why bread rises.

Is for technology, like using cool kitchen gadgets to make cooking fun and easy, from tools to tablets.

Is for engineering, like being a food builder and inventor, creating tasty food structures, and solving food puzzles.

Is for art, like making meals colorful and beautiful by using food like paint to create edible masterpieces.

Is for mathematics, like using numbers to make food taste just right, counting, measuring, and cooking with math magic!

So, put on your Food Explorer hat, let curiosity be your guide, and flip the page to start your adventure!

Anatomy of a Food Explorer

Sensory Superpower
I explore food in fun ways: seeing, touching, hearing, smelling, and tasting.

Discover-Me Badges
I celebrate my food adventures, as they honor my curiosity and the joy of discovering with every exploration.

Kindness Compass
I learn to share, care, and play fair with my friends, enjoying our food adventures together.

Thankful Heart
I share happy food moments with family and friends, finding foods that are just right for me.

iSpy Binoculars
I spot fun food adventures from far, finding new foods and cool places to explore, each peek bringing me closer to surprises.

Curiosity Cape
I learn and grow, becoming smarter as I explore new foods.

Wonder Books
I discover new foods, facts, and places; they are my pals, sharing tales and sparking my curiosity with each page.

Food Explorer Hat
I'm a food detective, uncovering food mysteries and enjoying fun discoveries on my journey.

Discovery Map
I journey to new places, exploring the different foods and flavors of people and their cultures from around the world.

YumZoomer
I use the magnifying glass to see the tiny secrets of food and discover its hidden stories.

Investigation Journal
I write clues, draw food pictures, think about, and remember fun food stories I discover.

Adventure Backpack
I have everything I need for food adventures, ready to share my new discoveries!

Memory Maker
I capture the fun of each food adventure, saving the best moments and discoveries to share and remember.

Explorer Boots
I step into food adventures, tiptoe into experiments, and dance through discoveries.

Food Explorers come in all sorts of shapes, sizes, colors, backgrounds, and abilities, and each one is as unique as a red apple in a green orchard. There's no one 'right' way to explore because we all have our own favorite things and feelings about food. So, pick what you love from this list, and let your curiosity guide you. This adventure is yours to make your own.

Food Explorer's Oath

I, _____ am a Food Explorer; ready to hop, skip, and jump into the world of food with an open heart and a curious mind.

As a Food Explorer, I will:

Explore with Curiosity: Be a food detective, asking questions and uncovering mysteries about food.

Be Courageous: Make food an adventure, investigating and bravely trying new foods in ways that feel safe to me.

Grow in Confidence: Learn to trust my amazing body, find what makes me feel my best, and let others know what I need.

Unleash My Creativity: Use my imagination to have food-filled fun through activities like science experiments, art projects, and kitchen adventures that spark my interest.

Stay Open-minded: Use my senses to explore foods, discover diverse cultures, and welcome the magic of learning about people from around the world.

Respect All Tastes: Understand that everyone has foods they like, and it's perfectly okay if we all like different things.

Spread Kindness: Use food to show love and support by cooking together with friends, going on food adventures, and celebrating delicious meals.

Team Up: Work as a team with my food explorer friends, having loads of fun and learning together.

Practice Safety: Always have a grown-up helper in the kitchen and wherever I explore food, using my food tools with care and responsibility.

Be Earth-Friendly: Learn how to take care of our planet by making thoughtful choices, like reducing waste and recycling when I can.

And most importantly, **I PROMISE** to have loads of **fun** and make awesome **memories**!

By making this promise, I am lacing up my explorer boots, ready to embark on exciting food adventures and explore the wonderful world of food!

FOOD EXPLORER'S CODE

We, the Food Explorers, carry our promise in our hearts and actions. Our code reminds us of our commitment to food exploration, curiosity, kindness, and responsibility. Our adventures are filled with laughter and fun while we make memories learning about the amazing world of food.

As Food Explorers, we:

Embrace Curiosity: We ask questions, explore the mysteries of food, and keep our curious minds wide open.

Embody Courage: We bravely embark on delicious adventures, fearlessly trying new foods that feel safe.

Cultivate Confidence: We trust our incredible bodies, discover what makes us feel our best, and express our needs with confidence.

Spark Creativity: We unleash our imagination to have food-filled fun, from kitchen experiments to artful creations.

Champion Open-mindedness: We use our senses to explore diverse foods, cultures, and learn about people from all over the world.

Respect Every Taste: We understand that everyone has their favorite foods, and we celebrate our differences.

Spread Kindness: We use food to show love and support, cooking and sharing with friends, and spreading joy.

Team Up: We work together as a team, having fun and learning from one another.

Prioritize Safety: With the help of grown-ups, we always ensure safety in the kitchen and during food exploration, using our tools the right way.

Care for the Earth: We learn to make eco-friendly choices, reducing waste and recycling, to protect our planet.

By following our **Food Explorers Code**, we celebrate food, culture, and friendship, and we turn every food adventure into a delicious journey of discovery and fun!

YOU choose your adventures in food!

scientific method

STEP 1: LOOK AROUND
Begin your adventure in the Observation Orchard, where you can look closely at different foods. What curious things do you see? Does something make you go "hmm?"

Observation Orchard

1

STEP 2: ASK AWAY
Next, visit the Wondering Woods, where you can think of questions about the foods you saw. What do you wonder about?

2

Wondering Woods

STEP 3: FIND OUT
Now, head to the Discovery Den, where you can look in books, ask grown-ups, or use a computer to find answers to your questions. It's like being a detective looking for clues!

3

Discovery Den

STEP 4: TAKE A GUESS
Climb up to Hypothesis Hill where you can make a smart guess called a hypothesis about your question. A hypothesis is like whispering a secret answer to a question and then doing a fun experiment to see if your secret whisper was right. What do you think the answer might be?

4

Hypothesis Hill

Welcome to your Food Explorer Discovery Map— it's like a special treasure map that helps you uncover the secrets of food with the help of something called the 'scientific method.' Think of it as a compass that leads the way for Food Explorers! Every time you're curious about something, that's where your adventure begins.

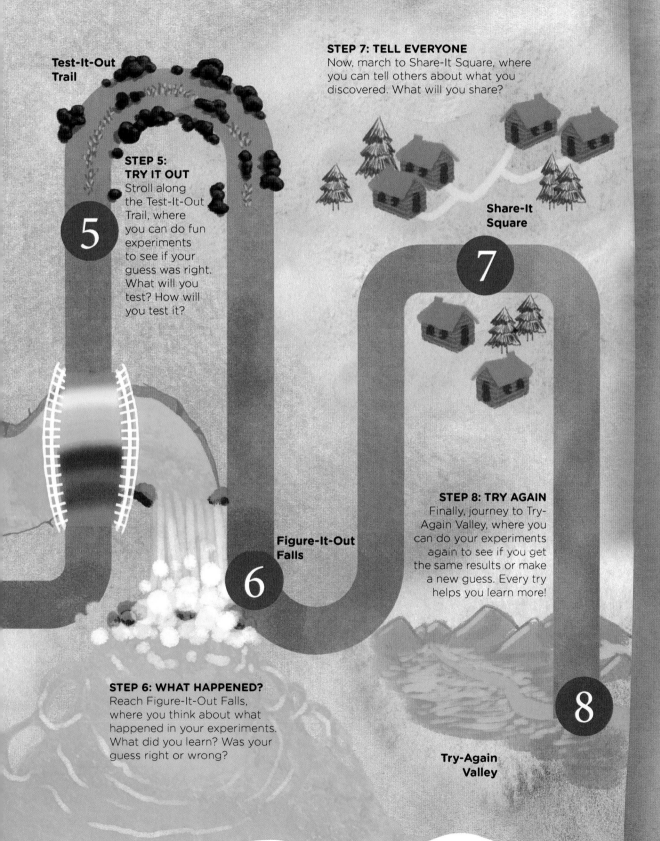

Test-It-Out Trail

STEP 7: TELL EVERYONE
Now, march to Share-It Square, where you can tell others about what you discovered. What will you share?

STEP 5: TRY IT OUT
Stroll along the Test-It-Out Trail, where you can do fun experiments to see if your guess was right. What will you test? How will you test it?

Share-It Square

Figure-It-Out Falls

STEP 8: TRY AGAIN
Finally, journey to Try-Again Valley, where you can do your experiments again to see if you get the same results or make a new guess. Every try helps you learn more!

STEP 6: WHAT HAPPENED?
Reach Figure-It-Out Falls, where you think about what happened in your experiments. What did you learn? Was your guess right or wrong?

Try-Again Valley

Fiddlehead Fern

Brussels Sprouts

Basil

Nopal

Invite friends to a virtual cook-along to make a broccoli dish together.

Broccoli

Pistachio Icecream

Guacamole

Leek

Lime

Squeeze a lime and
measure how much
juice you collected.

OLIVES Put on a puppet show with olives on your fingers.

Line up cucumbers like dominoes, then watch them tumble down.

Learn about fermentation, then make sauerkraut from cabbage.

Cabbage

CUCUMBER

ARTICHOKE

KOHLRABI

Edamame

GREEN

Did you know plants need food to grow? Green is a magical color for plants thanks to a helper called chlorophyll. Chlorophyll [chlo-ro-phyll] is like a tiny green chef that uses sunlight to cook up food for the plant. When the sun shines, chlorophyll gets to work, turning light into yummy food that helps the plant grow big and strong. So cool! As you explore the green foods on this page, can you guess which ones have chlorophyll? When you taste-test green plants, you are tasting the same food that nourish the plant's growth, and now it's nourishing you too!

spinach

PEas

POMELO

CORN

Create a doll from corn husks and silks.

STAR FRUIT

Design "You are a star!" stickers with cool starfruit pictures.

EGGS

CHEESE

Look for shapes in food like the oval in an eggshell and the round yolk.

CHERRIES

MANGO

JACKFRUIT

Pineapple

Pasta

Kiwano Melon

Peach

Make colorful pasta jewelry with paint and elastic bands.

YELLOW

Did you know bananas love playing dress-up? When they are young, they wear green coats. But as they grow older and become sweeter, they change into bright yellow outfits. And guess what? When they are fully ripe, they add brown speckles to their yellow jackets, like sprinkles on a cake! This magical transformation is thanks to a special gas called ethylene [eth-uh-leen], which helps bananas ripen and taste sweeter. Delicious! As you explore the yellow foods on this page, can you spot others that might go through a similar ripening process? Which foods do you think change as they ripen, just like bananas do?

Physalis

Banana

Observe how bananas ripen in a brown paper bag versus on the counter.

Nachos

Lemon

TORTILLA

Create a picture recipe card for making tortillas with step-by-step instructions.

Jícama

naan

CRACKERS

Build a towering stack of crackers using nut butter or cheese.

BREAD

Slice toast into triangles to make a tangram puzzle, then solve it.

FRIES

oats

potato

Make a Mr. Potato Head with googly eyes and craft supplies.

walnuts

onion

cashews

Tan

Have you ever wondered how bread is made? It begins as a squishy, tan dough with simple ingredients like flour and water, but many breads have a special helper called yeast [ye-st]. Yeast helps the dough rise and creates a light, spongy texture. When you warm up bread to make crispy toast, listen to the crackling song it sings as it heats up. That sound is the tiny water droplets inside the bread turning into steam and dancing their way out! As you explore the tan foods on this page, can you spot any other foods that may have started as dough? Do you think they are made with yeast?

cheerios

muffin

Bake muffins with and without baking powder and see what changes.

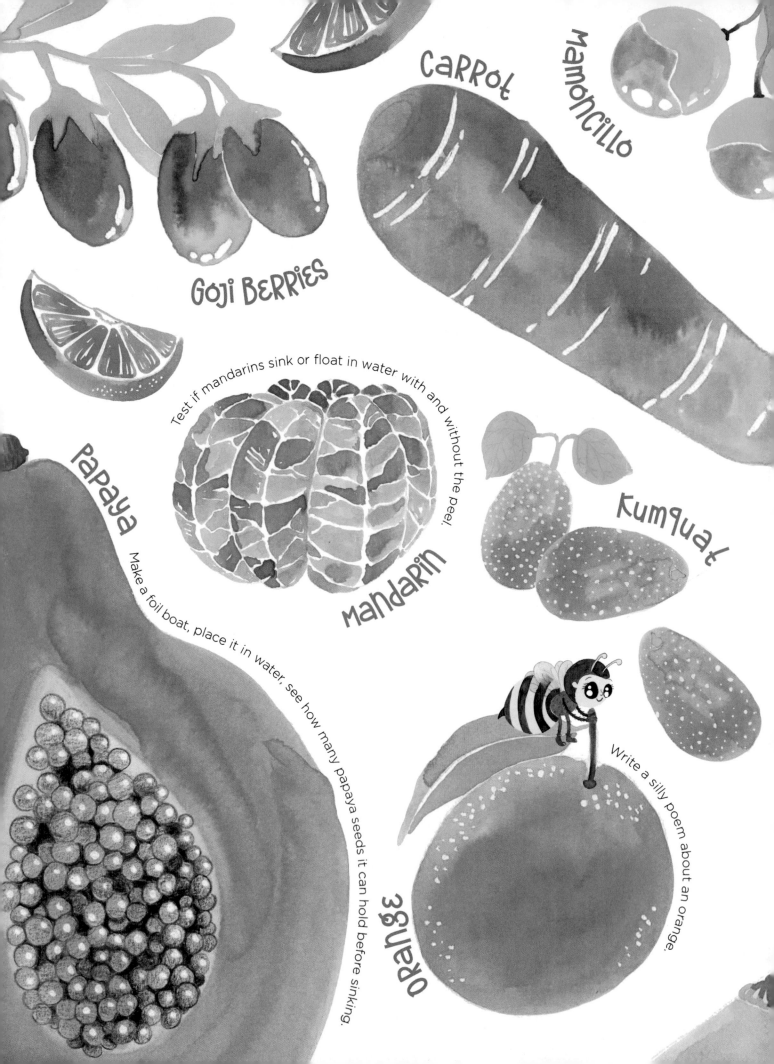

MaMONCiLLO

CaRROt

GOJi BERRiES

Test if mandarins sink or float in water with and without the peel.

PaPaYa

MaNDaRiN

KumQuat

Make a foil boat, place it in water, see how many papaya seeds it can hold before sinking.

Write a silly poem about an orange.

ORaNGe

Passion Fruit

Butternut squash

Use a tablet to look for a butternut squash recipe to make.

Persimmon

Cantaloupe

ORANGE

Have you ever wondered why a color and a fruit have the same name? Before being named after the sweet and juicy fruit, the color was called yellow-red. But here's a fun twist: oranges are actually green when they grow in warm places! They wear a coat of green thanks to chlorophyll (the tiny green helper we learned about on the green foods page!). But when the weather gets chilly, the green coat disappears and the beautiful orange color underneath shines through. So cool! As you explore the orange foods on this page, can you guess which ones have changed colors as they ripened, just like orange fruit? Which orange foods on this page have you taste-tested?

Sweet Potato

Candy corn

Use candy corn to play with adding and taking away.

TAMARIND

Pick a curious food like tamarind, then learn how it is eaten around the world.

BREAD

Coconut

Craft a birdfeeder from a coconut shell, then hang it with string.

Slice a kiwi into round pieces, then slice like a pizza to see parts of a whole.

Kiwi

PRETZEL

HamBurGer

Sapodilla

Almonds

sapote

meatballs

Dates

Make a musical shaker with dried date pits in a plastic bottle.

BROWN

Did you know that chocolate comes from a fruit? It's made from the cacao [ca-cow] beans tucked inside the fruit pods of the cacao tree. These beans go on a big adventure: they are fermented, dried, roasted, ground, mixed, heated, and then cooled to become velvety chocolate. Long ago, chocolate was a bitter drink, but now, with a sprinkle of sugar and a splash of milk, it's a sweet treat we love in many forms. As you explore the brown foods on this page, you're diving into a world of sweet transformations. Can you spot any brown foods on this page that you think would taste yummy with chocolate?

Pecans

chocolate

Place dark, milk, and white chocolate on a hot plate and see which one melts first.

taro

Salami

MiRaCle BeRRies

Tomato

Explore tomato varieties and the differences in seeds, juice, and texture.

Radish

Red KidNey BeaNs

Craft a rainbow collage using colorful dried beans.

BELL PEPPER

RaspBeRRies

WateRmeloN Use a watermelon rind as a tunnel for small cars and zoom them through.

SAUSAGE

CRANBERRIES

CURRANTS

Take daily pictures of a
strawberry plant, then combine
them into a fast video.

POMEGRANATE

STRAWBERRIES

Gummy WORMS

Red

Did you know red is a magical color? It's like a signal
from nature! Sometimes it warns us of spicy foods like
hot red chili peppers or zesty radishes. But it also invites
us to enjoy sweet ripe fruits like strawberries and red
apples. Yum! Every red food has a story. By exploring
them, you're learning their colorful tales. As you look at
the red foods on this page, can you guess which ones
are fiery hot and which ones are sweet treats ready to
be taste-tested? Which red foods are new to you?

APPLE

CHILI PEPPER

Make up a math story about chilies growing in a garden.

LOLLIPOP

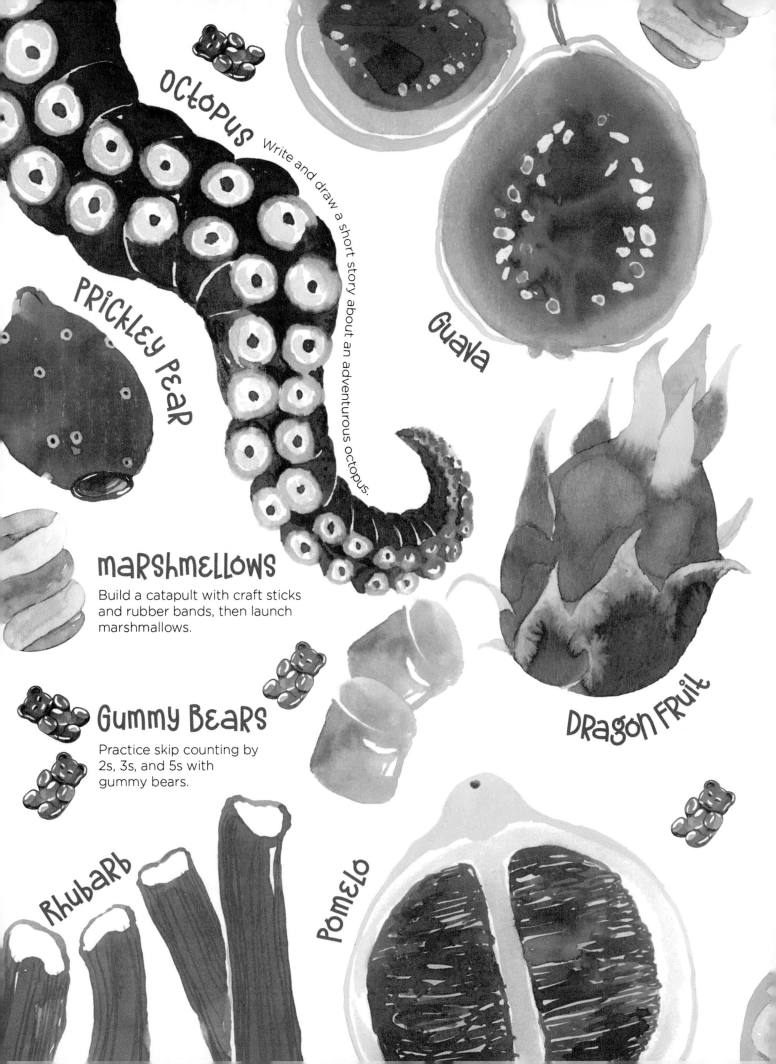

OCtOPUS

Write and draw a short story about an adventurous octopus.

PRiCKLEY PEaR

Guava

DRaGon FRuit

marshmellows

Build a catapult with craft sticks and rubber bands, then launch marshmallows.

Gummy BEaRS

Practice skip counting by 2s, 3s, and 5s with gummy bears.

RhubaRb

Pomεlo

salmon

lychee

Make a video showing how to eat a lychee.

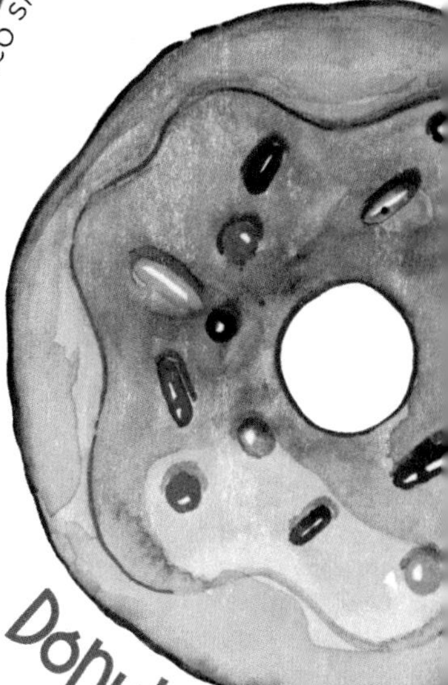

Donut

Pink

Did you know every fruit begins as a flower? The magic starts when tiny friends like bees and butterflies visit them, carrying special dust called 'pollen.' This amazing process is called pollination [pol-li-na-tion], and it transforms flowers into delicious fruits. With a magnifying glass in a garden, you can see this magic up close! As you explore the pink fruits on this page, you're stepping into nature's wonder. Which pink fruits have you taste-tested?

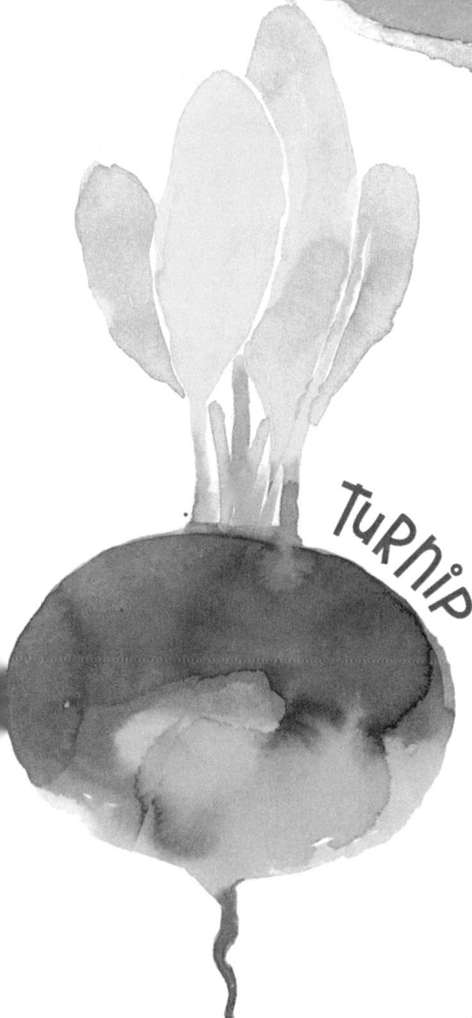

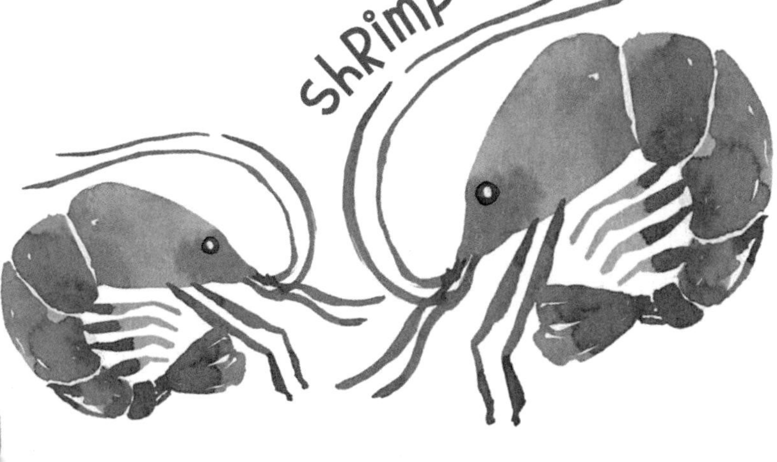

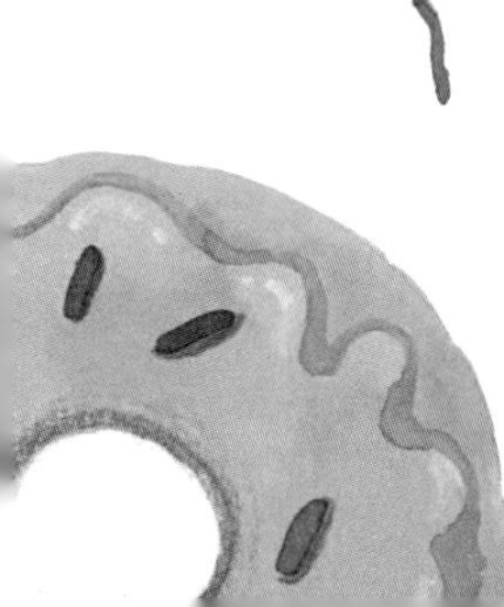

TuRnip

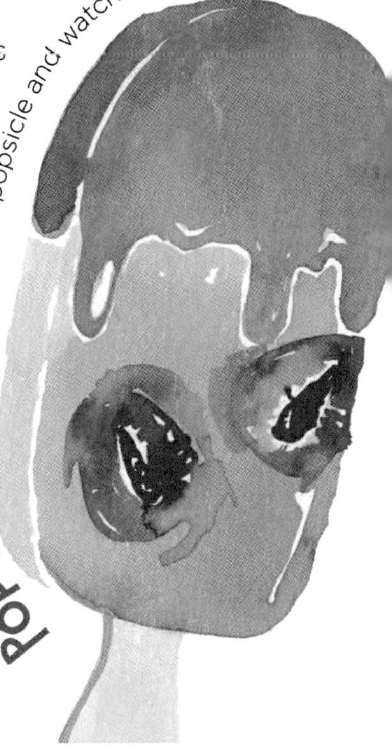

shRimp

Popsicle

Sprinkle salt on a popsicle and watch what happens.

SWEET POTATO

BEET

Create temporary tattoos using beetroot slices and cookie cutters.

Figs

Passion Fruit

cauliflower

caRRot

Use the internet to learn why the first carrots were grown.

JELLO

Make edible gelatin blocks, then use them to build something fun.

ASPaRagus

Weigh different veggies like cabbage and line them up from lightest to heaviest.

manGosteen

Radicchio

PuRPLe

Learn about plums and why they are called "stone fruit."

Have you ever wondered how purple foods get their purple color? The natural color in food comes from something known as pigments. Purple foods like plums, eggplants, and purple cabbage get their beautiful color from a group of natural pigments called anthocyanins. Try saying the word out loud, it's pronounced "an-tho-cy-a-nins." These pigments are not just pretty to look at, they also help our bodies grow and fight off sickness. As you explore the purple foods on this page, can you guess which ones have anthocyanins?

PLum

GRaPes

eGGPlant

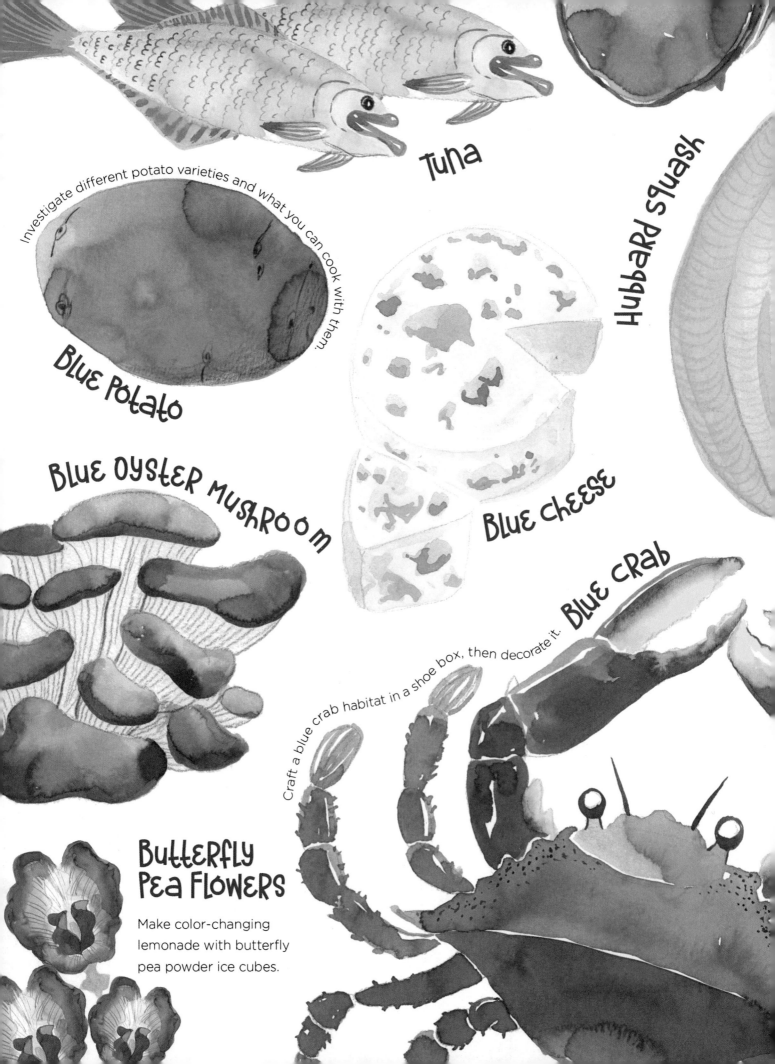

Tuna

Hubbard Squash

Investigate different potato varieties and what you can cook with them.

Blue Potato

Blue Cheese

Blue Oyster Mushroom

Blue Crab

Craft a blue crab habitat in a shoe box, then decorate it.

Butterfly Pea Flowers

Make color-changing lemonade with butterfly pea powder ice cubes.

Damson Plum

Blue Turmeric

Compare the lengths of different squash, then line them up from shortest to longest.

Blue

Blue is a curious color in the food world, don't you think? It does not show up on our plates often, but when it does, it brings a fun surprise like blue cheese. This cheese gets its blue-marbled designs from a friendly mold called Penicillium. Try saying the word out loud, it's pronounced "pen-uh-sil-ee-uhm." It's like a little artist that paints strong, zesty flavors and cool blue patterns on the cheese as it ages over time. Blue cheese brings its bold taste crumbled on salads and fancy cheese trays. As you peek at the blue foods on this page, do the blue hues make them look yummy or not so good? Can you find a blue food you want to taste-test?

Blueberries

Take a picture of a blueberry, then turn it into a silly character using photo editing.

Concord Grapes

BLACKBERRIES

Make edible finger paint with blackberries and instant vanilla pudding.

ELDERBERRIES

OREO COOKIE

Open a package of Oreos and sort whole cookies from broken pieces.

SUNFLOWER SEEDS

MULBERRIES

CHERRIES

Invent a tool for pitting cherries using kitchen items.

Chia

Tomato

PEPPER

Black Radish

Açai

Go on a virtual field trip to see how acai berries grow on a farm.

BLACK

Did you know black pepper is actually a tiny "stone fruit," just like cherries and peaches? These small fruits are picked while they are still green and unripe. As they dry, they transform from green to black, revealing a spicy, earthy flavor that wakes up our taste buds. It's like they're playing hide-and-seek with their spicy flavor until they're ready to be found. As you explore the black foods on this page, think about the magical transformations they might be hiding. Each black food has a tale of transformation, waiting to be discovered. Which food will you explore first?

Raisins

Watch a grape dry into a raisin over time.

TRUFFLES

OLives

NoRi

caviaR

white Beans

Fennel

Milk

Pretend to be a food critic, then review dairy, coconut, and oat milk in a video.

Cheese

Tofu

Cauliflower

yogurt

Hearts of Palm

Water Chestnut

Cupcake

Decorate cupcakes with colorful frosting, sprinkles, and fruit.

Practice measuring with rice using different sizes of measuring cups.

Rice

Popcorn

Turn a cardboard box into a popcorn stand for movie night.

White

White is a color full of surprises! Did you know that white light is made of all the colors of the rainbow? But with foods like cauliflower, white means there's no color at all. Cauliflower stays white because it grows under big green leaves, hiding from the sun's color-changing rays. But guess what? Cauliflower can also come in fun colors like purple, orange, and green! As you explore the white foods on this page, can you find other foods that come in many colors too?

Daikon

Asparagus

Learn why some asparagus are white, and some are green.

Mushrooms

Use a magnet to find iron in cereal, then explore its magnetic properties.

Investigate different potato varieties and ways to cook them.

Observe how fruits ripen differently in a brown paper bag versus on the counter.

Put dark, milk, and white chocolate on a hot plate and see which one melts first.

Explore different varieties of the same fruit or veggie and spot the differences.

SCIENCE

Have you ever wondered how rainbows are made or how a tiny seed grows into a big tree? That's the magic of science – it's all about being curious and discovering new things! Anyone can be a scientist - you can start by asking questions about the world around you and doing fun experiments to find the answers. Every time you wonder, ask questions, and explore, like when you try out activities from this page, you are diving into the amazing world of science!

Slice up fruits like apples and bananas, then investigate why they turn brown.

Learn about different types of fruit like simple, aggregate, and multiple fruit.

Put gummy bears in water and watch how they grow throughout the day.

Pop marshmallows in the microwave and watch them puff up really big.

Bake muffins with and without baking powder and see what changes.

Drop different fruits and veggies in water and see if they sink or float.

Layer liquids like honey and water in a jar to see how they stack.

Discover why some asparagus are white and others are green.

Sprinkle salt on ice or a popsicle and observe what happens.

Dissolve an eggshell in vinegar and make the egg bounce.

Mix sugar in hot and cold water to notice the difference.

Try tasting food while blindfolded, then guess the food.

Learn about fermentation and create fermented food.

Find out why popcorn pops when it gets hot.

Watch a grape dry into a raisin over time.

Learn how seedless fruits are grown.

TECHNOLOGY

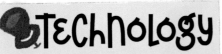

Have you ever wondered how video games are made or how a robot knows what to do? That's the magic of technology – it's all about creating cool tools and gadgets that make our lives easier and more fun. Anyone can be a technologist - you can start by asking questions about the gadgets and gizmos around you and doing fun projects to see how they work. Every time you wonder, ask questions, and explore, like when you try out activities from this page, you are diving into the exciting world of technology!

Make a 2-week picture menu for easy lunchbox packing.

Record a video showing how to eat something unusual.

Record kitchen sounds like crunching chips and sizzling frying, then turn it into a guessing game.

Go on a virtual shopping trip using a grocery app and add favorite snacks to the cart.

Join a class to learn how to take good food pictures.

Make an animated food story using an app.

Use a tablet to look for a recipe to make.

Pretend to be a chef on a cooking show and teach how to make a simple dish.

Take pictures of food, then turn them into silly characters using photo editing.

Invite friends to a virtual cook-along to make a favorite recipe together.

Take daily pictures of a garden, then combine them into a fast video.

Bring a calculator to the grocery store and add up the food costs.

Pretend to be a food critic, then make a video review of a meal.

Use the internet to learn about food from different countries.

Design a chart or checklist to keep track of foods to explore.

Learn about the history of a favorite food using the internet.

Make a pretend restaurant menu on a computer or tablet.

Create a recipe card with step-by-step picture instructions.

Create a kitchen scavenger hunt game.

Go on a virtual field trip to visit a farm.

Design stickers with cool food pictures.

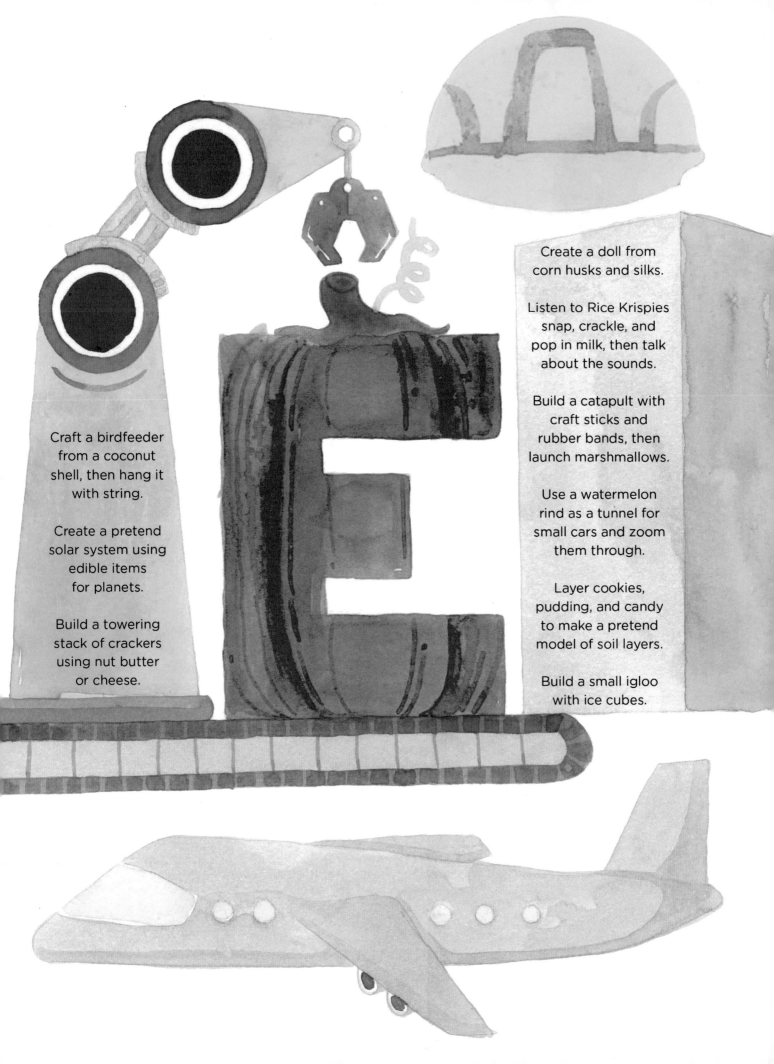

Craft a birdfeeder from a coconut shell, then hang it with string.

Create a pretend solar system using edible items for planets.

Build a towering stack of crackers using nut butter or cheese.

Create a doll from corn husks and silks.

Listen to Rice Krispies snap, crackle, and pop in milk, then talk about the sounds.

Build a catapult with craft sticks and rubber bands, then launch marshmallows.

Use a watermelon rind as a tunnel for small cars and zoom them through.

Layer cookies, pudding, and candy to make a pretend model of soil layers.

Build a small igloo with ice cubes.

Craft little boats from foil to see how many papaya seeds each boat can hold before sinking.

Cut food into shapes with cookie cutters, then put them back together like puzzle pieces.

Make a flour maze on a baking sheet, then blow a small candy through it with a straw.

Transform a cardboard box into a lemonade stand, then pretend to sell lemonade.

engineering

Have you ever wondered how bridges stay up or how skyscrapers touch the sky? That's the magic of engineering – it's all about using your imagination to solve puzzles and build things that help us in our daily lives! Anyone can be an engineer - you can start by asking questions about the structures and machines around you and doing fun projects to see how they work. Every time you wonder, ask questions, and explore, like when you try out activities from this page, you are diving into the surprising world of engineering!

Make a self-watering system for plants using plastic bottles.

Turn fruits and veggies into race cars, then race them.

Line up food like dominoes, then watch them fall.

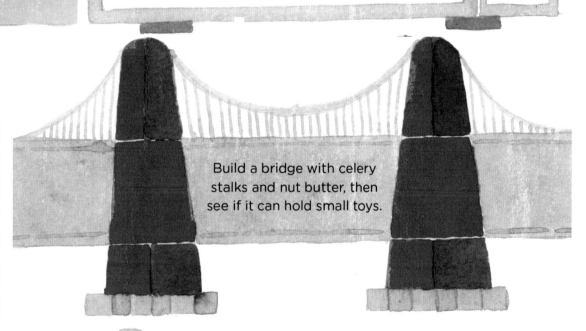

Build a bridge with celery stalks and nut butter, then see if it can hold small toys.

Invent a new helpful tool for the kitchen using things around the house.

Make an animal home in a shoe box and decorate it like a real habitat.

Build the tallest tower with uncooked spaghetti and marshmallows.

Make edible gelatin blocks, then use them to build something fun.

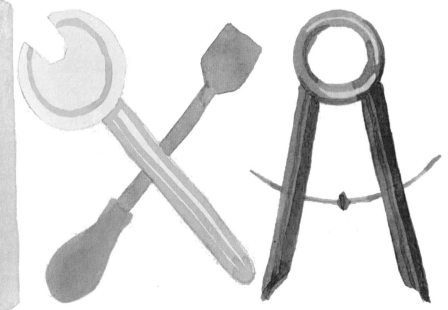

Create Mr. Potato Head with a real potato, googly eyes, and craft supplies.

Craft a fruit bouquet with cookie cutter-shaped fruit on skewers in a vase.

Mix up edible finger paint using blackberries and instant vanilla pudding.

Arrange a colorful fruit or vegetable platter into an edible masterpiece.

Create color-changing lemonade with butterfly pea powder ice cubes.

Put on a finger puppet show using raspberries.

Draw a picture of a family food tradition.

Make up a song about a favorite food.

Write a silly poem about food.

Make a musical shaker with dried cherry pits in a plastic bottle.

Personalize an apron or chef hat with fabric markers or paint.

Decorate cupcakes with colorful frosting, sprinkles, and fruit.

Draw a favorite meal and describe its flavors and textures.

Make colorful pasta jewelry with paint and elastic bands.

Design food-themed bookmarks with colorful drawings.

Design a placemat, decorate it, then get it laminated.

Craft a rainbow picture using colorful dried lentils.

Make pizza into a work of art with colorful toppings.

Create a fun dance using a food item as a prop.

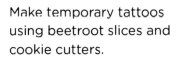

Write and draw a short story about a food adventure.

Make temporary tattoos using beetroot slices and cookie cutters.

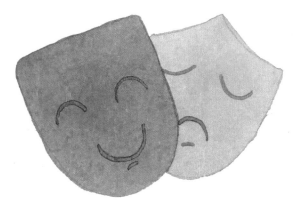

ARt

Have you ever wondered how a cartoon is made or how your favorite book was written? That's the magic of art – it's all about using your imagination and creativity to make your ideas real! Anyone can be an artist - you can start by asking questions about the colors, shapes, and stories around you and doing fun projects to make your vision come true in pictures, stories, or songs. Every time you wonder, ask questions, and explore, like when you try out activities from this page, you are diving into the colorful world of art!

Look for shapes in food, like circles in cucumber slices and squares in crackers.

Slice a pizza or break a chocolate bar to see how a whole is made of parts.

Set up a pretend market with a register to have fun with counting money and understanding its value.

Compare prices of the same food from two different brands at the store to see which one costs less.

Craft a bar graph to compare the number of snack pieces in two packages and see which has more.

Make a guess on the number of berries in a plastic container, then count them.

MathEmatics

Have you ever wondered how much of each ingredient is needed to bake chocolate chip cookies or if you have enough money to buy a new toy? That's the magic of math – it's all about solving puzzles and discovering the patterns that make our world work! Anyone can be a mathematician - you can start by asking questions about the numbers, shapes, and patterns around you and doing fun activities finding patterns and solving puzzles. Every time you wonder, ask questions, and explore, like when you try out activities from this page, you are diving into the awesome world of math!

Weigh different veggies and line them up from lightest to heaviest.

Pour water into different-sized cups, then compare the amounts with a measuring cup.

Bake cookies with a grown-up, talking about each step from start to finish.

Craft a tangram puzzle using cheese slices cut into triangles and squares.

Create a cereal number line, then count forward and backward along it.

Line up foods from shortest to longest, then measure how long they are.

Use a kitchen clock to see how long until mealtime or to time a recipe.

Slice fruit in half, then explore how they look the same on both sides.

Count the seeds inside different fruits, then compare the amounts.

Create patterns with fruit on a plate for a fun fruit snack-tivity.

Use candies or small fruits to practice adding and taking away.

Use candy or small fruit to skip count by 2s, 3s, and 5s.

Squeeze a citrus fruit and measure the juice collected.

Create a math story or math word problem with food.

Sort food by colors, shapes, and sizes.

Visit our Adventure Toolbox™ at www.kidfoodexplorers.com to download printables and resources.

Unlock a world of wonder and learning that starts in your kitchen! Access your free companion guide for STEAM Powered Food Adventures. It's packed with curiosity-sparking prompts and engaging activities tailored for kids age 4+. Start exploring now – Download your guide!

DISCOVER MORE!

Becoming a Food Explorer
A transformative rhyming adventure fostering a growth mindset around food for kids 4+.

Where Do Bananas Come From?
Discover, learn, and cook with a comprehensive fruit encyclopedia for kids 4+.

Where Does Broccoli Come From?
Discover, learn, and cook with a comprehensive vegetable encyclopedia for kids 4+.

A to Z with Fruits and Veggies
Master the ABCs with playful mini-stories featuring global fruits and veggies for kids ages 3-6.

101 Descriptive Words
Expand food-related vocabulary with a visual book featuring 101 descriptive words for kids ages 3-8.

My Food Explorer Mat & Comparison Mat
Grow adventurous eaters with a hands-on, child-led, taste-testing tool that will transform mealtimes for kids 3+.